LETTY'S
DO OR DIE COURAGE

March 2020

PAT LAUB

LETTY'S DO OR DIE COURAGE

Orders by U.S. trade bookstores and wholesalers. Email info@BeyondPublishing.net

The Beyond Publishing Speakers Bureau can bring authors to your live event. For more information or to book an event contact the Beyond Publishing Speakers Bureau speak@BeyondPublishing.net

The Author can be reached directly at BeyondPublishing.net

Manufactured and printed in the United States of America distributed globally by BeyondPublishing.net

New York | Los Angeles | London | Sydney

ISBN Hardcover: 978-1-952884-20-7

FROM THE AUTHOR

The days, months and years went by as I pushed forward to find a solution to rescuing a family of five from a war-torn country. Hearing the world news every day of the evolution in El Salvador only fueled me to work harder. Through prayer I felt God opening doors to accomplish this mission. I took a leap of faith and encouraged the family to escape their homeland and come to this country, that God would make a way.

It is my desire the reader will feel inspired to reach out and want to help others in need. This experience changed my life. It only takes one person. The rewards are immeasurable.

I want to thank my publisher Michael D. Butler for encouraging me to finish the story.

Pat Laub

CIVIL WAR IN
EL SALVADOR

At the beginning of 1980, thousands perished. Archbishop Oscar Romero was shot to death. Four U.S. Catholic Church workers were raped and murdered. Six Jesuit priests, their housekeeper, and her daughter were shot to death as military death-squads wiped out entire villages. This civil war lasted 12 years.

In September 1980, the five major, leftist revolutionary organizations merged to form Farabundo Marti National Liberation Front (FMLN). The FMLN fielded a guerilla army to oppose government and right-wing paramilitary forces.

This is a story of a courageous young mother who left her son and siblings to go to the U.S.A. to secure employment and provide for her family in El Salvador. However, there were no jobs to be had. The government had closed businesses down, due to the war. All able-bodied men were drafted into the army.

***

While driving home from Yosemite with my family, I began to plan my schedule for the next day. We had been away from home for a week, which meant a lot of laundry needed to be done.

The next morning, my husband left early for work, to prepare for a court hearing for his client. My plan was to stay home and do loads of laundry. After I showered, I was ready to tackle the dirty clothes, but the phone rang. I was needed at the office to fill in for the receptionist who had reported in sick. The laundry would have to wait.

While I was driving into the office, it started to rain heavily. Thankfully, I found a parking space close to the front door. I was just starting to settle in at the desk when two women came in the front door. They were both drenched from the rain. One of the women was Caucasian and the other was Hispanic. I introduced myself to them. The Caucasian woman's name was Pam. She asked if we could go someplace private to talk. I led the two ladies into a small office, and we all sat down. Pam introduced me to Letty, a petite, Hispanic woman with large, brown eyes and a beautiful smile.

Pam began to tell Letty's story. After sharing how Letty had come to this country, and the hardships she had endured while traveling to the U.S.A., Pam wanted to know if I would be interested in having a live-in housekeeper. Letty did not speak any English. This was a red flag. How in the world would I communicate? Her former employer had spoken Spanish.

Pam told me Letty was originally from El Salvador. She had been living and working in Los Angeles. She and her boyfriend had left El Salvador to escape the civil war. He then became physically and mentally abusive. Letty had arrived to work different times with bruises on her face. The breaking point for Letty was when he fractured her arm.

Pam told me that Letty's employer had feared for Letty's life. Letty had needed to leave the area and escape from the abusive man, and she had temporarily gone to stay with Pam. Pam had been searching for over a week and was getting desperate, as she had no prospects. Pam told me she liked Letty and her eagerness to pitch in and clean, even though Pam couldn't pay Letty. Pam continued to share how Letty's cleaning skills were excellent, and she loved children. I was listening and thinking, "I would like a live-in, but one who spoke English."

I told Pam I would talk to my husband. I knocked on the door and went in as he was loading his briefcase for court. I told him about Letty, and he reminded me we had three kids in college, plus a young child at home, and we couldn't afford to take care of one more person in the house. I agreed with him and went to tell Pam. She asked, "Do you have an extra bedroom? Or is it that he can't afford to pay Letty a salary?" I was silent. Pam asked if Letty could work for room and board. She was looking desperate, and Letty was smiling. While my husband walked through the small office space on his way to court, I told Pam, "My husband said no."

Pam stood up and headed for the door. Just as she turned the doorknob, I had this strong feeling to stop her. I called out, "Please wait! Come back in." I asked her how I could communicate with Letty since it would be difficult to do so. Pam assured me I could call when I needed to give Letty instructions.

Something came over me. I knew in my heart that this was the right thing to do. I didn't feel the need to know Letty's full story at that point. I told Pam I would give Letty a chance to work for me. I was in charge of my husband and my rentals in Berkley. I could pay Letty from my funds.

Now to figure out how to approach my husband... I knew I was going to be in trouble, but I felt this was the right decision to make. I grabbed my purse and coat and walked out the door to get Letty packed into my car. Letty was still smiling as Pam told her about living in my home.

When we arrived at home, we took her into my four-year-old Alicia's room. I moved Alicia to share my 14-year-old Dawn's room. I showed Letty where to hang her clothes, and I closed the door while she unpacked. Minutes later, she was in my kitchen, washing dishes. I made lunch for us. We then went to pick up Alicia from preschool. Letty was happy to see her, and Alicia began talking to her. Alicia was not happy that Letty didn't know how to answer her. We went grocery shopping and had errands to run. By the time we arrived home, it was time to make dinner. Letty was watching me as I began to peel potatoes, and she quickly found a knife to help. I put the plates and flatware out, and she set the table. I later learned that her previous employer had been a wealthy woman in L.A. who had spoken Spanish, and taught Letty how to cook and clean. We ate dinner, and then, I took Letty to her room and motioned for her to get ready for bed.

I used hand motions to tell her to stay in her room. My husband called to say he was on his way home. All afternoon, I had been praying for God to help me make this work out with my husband.

My husband arrived, and we had dinner. We then went upstairs to watch television. Somehow, I couldn't find the words to tell him I had brought Letty home to live with us. After going to bed, I prayed continuously. Eventually, I felt peaceful, relaxed, and had a restful night.

I woke up early, went downstairs, and found Letty in the laundry room, folding clothes. She had been washing and drying clothes for hours. The laundry was stacked neatly. I couldn't help myself—I raised my arms and gave her a hug. She beamed with delight.

I quickly motioned for her to go to her room, and I made her breakfast. I took it to her and put my finger to my lips to be quiet and closed the door.

Shortly thereafter, my husband came down for breakfast, carrying his briefcase. He grabbed a quick bite to eat and walked out the front door. All of a sudden, he quickly returned and said, "Who washed my car? It is spotless in and out!" I knew right away that Letty had gotten up at daybreak to clean his car. So, now was my chance to tell him.

"You know the lady you refused to let me hire yesterday? I hired her anyway, and she's the one who cleaned your car!"

All of a sudden, a big smile came across his face, and he clapped his hands and said, "She can stay!"

I laughed out loud, put my hands together, and said, "Thank you, God."

I was the property manager of our apartments in Berkley. My hours varied from four to six hours each day. Alicia loved Letty and wanted to stay home from preschool with her. Sometimes, when Letty had bad news, I would let her stay with Letty. She had a way of making Letty feel better. She was teaching Alicia Spanish. Before long, she and Letty could carry on a conversation. Sometimes, she would kneel with Letty and pray for her family.

Each day, Letty surprised me. One day, she was working in my rose garden and planting sweet peas. The next day, she was polishing the silver and vacuuming the furniture. The house had never been cleaner. She watched me cook, and before long, had memorized my recipes. Many days, she would already be making dinner for the family when I was running late. After Letty had lived with me for a few years, I learned to speak enough Spanish to ask her to start dinner. On Friday nights, we routinely had friends over. She knew what tablecloth to use and made centerpieces from roses from the garden and started dinners before I could ask. She was amazing.

She loved watching TV with Alicia—especially Sesame Street. Alicia taught her some English. From day one, I had made sure to pay her a salary. She was an angel sent to me to help make my life easier.

As time went by, I learned why she had come to California from El Salvador. She left her small son, her two sisters, her sister's baby, and her husband behind. Leaving her son, Alex, had been very sad for her. Her plan was to work and send money and clothes back to her family. As soon as the revolution was over, she would return.

On Sundays, Letty would get dressed up in her favorite dress to meet friends in San Francisco. There, she would purchase clothing and tennis shoes for her family.

Letty had to learn to send a single shoe at a time, rather than the pair. Otherwise, they would be stolen while in transit. She sent money orders to them. She loved taking photos of my family and sharing them with hers. As the time passed, I started to notice that she was becoming more saddened when she would receive letters from her family.

She became more nervous. I would hear her praying in the evening. I decided to purchase a Spanish Bible for her to read and believe in God's ability to protect her family. I compared my English Bible to the Spanish words. I shared with her to find the promises from Jesus—such as Hebrews 13:5, "I will never leave thee, nor forsake thee." I opened her eyes to how God had sacrificed His son to die on the cross for our sins, so we could have our sins forgiven and join Him in heaven. As she read the promises from Jesus, she began to believe in Jesus and hope for her family to be safe and someday join her in California. I prayed and requested prayers from my friends for Letty and her family.

Letty called Pam and asked me to listen while she translated one of the letters from Letty's family. This conversation helped me understand Letty's disposition. Sometimes, she was sad, and I had no idea why, unless I called Pam for the latest news of El Salvador. I could tell the conditions were continuing to get worse.

As the months went by, the village became more dangerous. The banditos were canvassing the homes, looking for men to force into their army. They had to either join or be killed. There was much difficulty in knowing when it was safe to go for food, supplies, or pick up mail from the post office. They knew the army scoured houses during all hours of the night and probably slept until noon the next day.

Letty's youngest sister went to Mass with a friend and her brother every week. She was considering becoming a nun. She was very dedicated to the Catholic Church and tithed her small portion of money given to her by Letty. Many times, she gave all of it to the church. She loved the priest and would help with housekeeping. But times were changing, and she felt fearful to attend church. Things were happening to villagers on their way to Mass. It was no longer safe.

Letty's two other sisters, Irma and Miriam, along with a few neighbor ladies, would walk into town once a week early in the day. The routine had continued until one day, they decided to shop for the children's Christmas presents. Just a few small items. It was near lunch, and they realized they had been shopping longer than planned. They quickly started back on the small dirt road to return home. While talking and discussing their purchases, several banditos suddenly came out of the jungle and began to attack them. While they were screaming and fighting back, the realization that they could be killed hit them. Irma screamed for everyone to give in and surrender to the attackers. After a long time of being abused, beaten, and raped, the abusers looked through their bags of groceries, took what they wanted, and left their victims naked and scared. Laying on the dirt, feeling sick and sobbing, they began to find their clothes, got dressed, and began to return home. They could no longer go shopping. The men would arm themselves and go for supplies and pick up mail and send letters to Letty.

I watched the news each evening. A lot of brutality continued to mount throughout most of El Salvador. I began to search out options to bring Letty's family to safety. I started with the Department of Immigration. They told me to apply for political asylum and agree to be Letty's sponsor for 20 years. I didn't need an appointment.

First, I went to San Francisco to find the immigration building. Once I found the right department, I saw a sea of people from all parts of the world, wanting to receive credentials to enter this country legally. I took my place in line. I spent a long time standing in line, and finally arrived at the window to find out I was in the wrong line. After spending most of the day there, I eventually had an application for Letty, and one for myself to be Letty's sponsor.

I returned home and called Pam to help me with the forms for Letty. The next day, I went back to the immigrations building and again waited in lines to present the completed forms. After an hour in line, the agent took the package, looked it over, and promised to get back to me by mail.

While waiting to hear from immigration, we got news of an attack at Letty's son's school. Alex, who was eight years old, had learned to play soccer and spent his spare time in the afternoons playing with friends. One day, while the boys were playing soccer after school, banditos surprised them in the distance. They had guns aimed at the boys. Alex saw them coming and yelled at his friends to run. Many were wounded and killed. Alex and one other boy ran into the jungle.

I returned home from work that day, and I could hear Letty crying loudly from inside the home. I immediately went to her, not understanding what had happened. She was shaking and tears were streaming down her face. I called Pam, and she told me Alex was missing. Now we needed to wait and pray for his safe return. I immediately went to get my Bible and came back to pray with Letty. I read the promises of God. She was still shaking, physically and emotionally distraught.

I called my family doctor, who had treated Letty for an ulcer. I told him about the bad news. He wrote a prescription to calm her nerves. I rushed to the pharmacy for the medicine and returned home. She took the medicine, while I warmed up a bowl of chicken soup. She probably had not eaten all day. After a while, the medicine began to work, and she was able to put food in her stomach. She reached for a blanket on the bed and wrapped herself up and laid down. I could see she had quit shaking and was soon sound asleep. She slept for 12 hours. While waiting for news of Alex, Letty spent most of her time on her knees praying.

At last, the phone rang, and I could hear Letty shouting with happiness. Alex had come out of the jungle with his friend. They had survived on fruit for three days. I could hear her voice change as she began to talk to Alex, her only child. Tears of joy ran down her cheeks.

The teachers, as a whole, did not support the revolution. Consequently, the banditos called for an assembly of teachers and students. While the students watched, their teachers were killed with machine guns. The trauma of this incident shook Alex, and he became very upset and fearful for his future.

For months, the family would pull up the floorboards in one small area in the house to take blankets under the house to sleep, and then, they would put the boards back down to not look suspicious.

I prayed for God to give me direction on what I could do to rescue this family. Their lives were on hold. There was no promise for tomorrow. They were living day to day, minute to minute.

I felt helpless to solve this situation. Yet, the urging of my spirit was to step out of my comfort zone. Considering I had not heard from the Department of Immigration, I decided to inquire about hiring an immigration attorney. I had to find out if there was any possible way to bring them here.

I met with two attorneys who had reputations of securing immigrants by political asylum. They both discouraged me, due to the political climate. President Carter had been misinformed about the civil war. He had not realized the magnitude of the problem in El Salvador until massive graves had been found. Political asylum was out of the question. At least, that was their opinion.

I saw no other option but to ask them to make an escape from El Salvador and go to Mexico. The family contacted a family member who lived in Mexico. Within hours, they had packed up and made their way to the small village. Shortly after their arrival, they were able to secure a house to rent. Doors began to open. Immediately, Alex was enrolled in school and the adults found jobs. I'm amazed how ambitious and driven they were.

Letty had saved for the future to help bring them to the U.S.A.—

or at least to Mexico. Each month, she mailed a money order to pay for their rent and groceries.

Letty was hoping and praying for the day when they could travel to San Diego, California. We waited for the political climate to be more sympathetic and compassionate to refugees relocating to California. While in Mexico, they were at least away from the fighting and killing in El Salvador. They didn't have to sleep underneath the floors with snakes and rats. Things had improved.

After two years of living and working in Mexico, I told them to pick a time to walk to the border. They located a man who promised them safe crossing into the San Diego region— for a price, of course. Letty was notified and wired the amount to them.

I saw God working in this plan. My husband surprised me with a birthday gift and reserved a week with friends to go to a health resort in Tecate, Mexico, near San Diego. Prior to leaving for Mexico, I had not heard about a scheduled time when the family was planning to cross the border.

I was in Tecate when I received an emergency call from my husband. He told me that Letty heard from her family and they had made it across the border. However, they had been picked up by the border patrol. They were in a holding area at the El Cid hotel in San Diego. The bad news was, they were scheduled to be sent back to El Salvador. He said, "I don't see a way out. They will have to go back."

I answered, "Oh no, I cannot let this happen. God will make a way. I will believe He will make a way. I believe God is in control. Where there's a will, there is a way."

He said, "Okay, I will help you any way I can. Keep me posted."

I found a San Diego phonebook and began to call immigration lawyers. I spent the whole day talking to lawyers referring me to other lawyers who specialized in immigration.

It was about 4:00 p.m. when I received a call from a lawyer by the name of Mr. Maurtino. I began to tell him Letty's story. I told him how they had been treated in El Salvador and had escaped near-death situations. Each night, they had crawled under the floor. I told him how the mom of the small toddler had had to hold her hand over his mouth, so he wouldn't make noise—in fear that the banditos would hear him. I told him about the different events the family had been through. He paused for a minute and explained he had just returned from Mexico from a four-year assignment, and normally, he would not take any new clients. He went on to say this would be a challenge due to the political climate, and how our government had made the decision to return all citizens from El Salvador back to their homeland. He also said he could not promise me he could make it happen.

But he agreed to take the case. With that news, I took a deep breath and told him this could make a difference in at least five people's lives. I thanked him. I noticed this heaviness that I had been carrying was starting to lift from my body. I felt we finally had a breakthrough! God was making this happen. I had new hope.

Mr. Maurtino asked for their names. He told me he would check the holding list and then call me back. Just as I hung up, my husband called me to report a very important message. He told me he had seen on the front page of the Oakland Tribune that anyone picked up migrating from El Salvador was being sent back, taken into the jungle, and killed.

In my small room, I knelt down and began to pray. I called the lawyer and told him the latest news, but he said he had not heard this and would work diligently to go the distance. As we spoke, he was going over the holding list, and it was difficult. It was a long list of people with the same last name. He asked me to repeat the names again. Finally, he had located the five people on the list. He told me there was bad news, and they were scheduled to be put on the plane by 5:00 p.m. the next day.

I felt we were under the gun to make this happen, and we had less than 24 hours to make the deadline. Otherwise, immigration planned to carry out the official order to get them on board the plane to El Salvador.

Mr. Maurtino would search the court calendar and find out who was hearing the case. He said he would try to contact the judge by phone right away. Otherwise, he would go to court in person first thing in the morning. He asked me to be available to appear with him in court. I prayed and trusted God would make this happen. At last, I felt things were happening in my favor. I was sure my mission was coming to fruition. I knelt at my bedside and began thanking God for granting my prayers. I rose up and got into bed. I felt myself letting go of the stress I had been holding onto for months. Not knowing what the outcome would be, I turned my fear over to God. In faith, I took some deep breaths and soon, I felt my body relax with peace of mind.

I awoke to the phone ringing. Mr. Maurtino called to say he had been able to reach the judge the last evening just before he left his office. After explaining the ordeal of the five family members, and the foreseeable future they could face, the judge listened intently and said he would make a final decision in court.

Mr. Maurtino said we needed to be in court at 11:00a.m., and requested I have my husband wire money from Western Union. I contacted my husband, and we agreed the funds would be withdrawn from our kids' college funds. This was our only option on such short notice. I quickly drove to Western Union and picked up the check. I arrived downtown San Diego at the courthouse early.

Mr. Maurtino met me on the court steps. We walked into the courtroom. The court clerk called Mr. Maurtino to come forward . He walked to the bench, and he and the judge spoke in low voices. After a brief conversation, they shook hands, and the clerk called my name to appear in front of the judge. Mr. Maurtino spoke to the judge regarding my intentions.

The judge asked me if I was willing to do a sponsorship for the five family members if they were granted political asylum for 10 years, with accordance to the law they would apply for citizenship and secure employment as soon as possible. Raising my right hand, I pledged to follow through with the request of the court.

The judge asked me to come forward and present the payment. I walked to the bench and handed it to him. He then asked me to sign a political asylum agreement, along with the sponsorship agreement for the next ten years. He handed me a large envelope with the valid papers stating each member had been granted political asylum, along with cards they were to carry with them at all times. We were dismissed and left the courtroom.

As we were leaving, I asked Mr. Maurtino what his fee was. He told me $5,000. I told him I would mail a check when I arrived at home. I continued to say how grateful I was for the outcome. He cleared his throat and said, "I wish more people would take the time and energy to reach out and help others, as you have done. I rarely do this, but I have decided to forgo charging you for my services. This is a gift I want to give to you and the family. I feel it is the right thing to do." In awe of his generosity, I thanked him again.

I was curious about something. I had sensed that he and the judge might have had a special friendship. I asked him if it was too confidential to talk about. He confirmed my suspicions and said they were close friends. He also said it had been a few years since he had been in his courtroom. The judge, his friend, had welcomed him back. Mr. Maurtino also shared that President Reagan had appointed him as the counsel general to Mexico for four years, and he had only been home 24 hours when an attorney friend had contacted him. I laughed and told him how I had searched the phonebook and called every attorney in San Diego who specialized in immigration law.

His attorney friend had told him my story and felt he was qualified to work on an emergency case with only hours left before the family would be returned to El Salvador. At that moment, I realized he had been appointed by God to take my case. This was truly answered prayers. God had made a way!

Mr. Maurtino shook my hand, handed me an address where the family was located, and told me that I could pick them up the next morning. I said goodbye and thanked him once again for making what had looked impossible, into reality. A dream come true.

I found a payphone and called my husband. I shared with him the news that we had made it happen! I went on to tell him the family had been granted political asylum. He complimented me and admitted that he hadn't thought it would ever happen. He had thought I was spinning my wheels.

I told my husband—who was not a Christian—that I serve a powerful God who can make things happen, if only we trust Him. He agreed it was a miracle. I ask him to make reservations for us to fly home, and I gave him the names of the family for their plane reservations. He wished me happy birthday. I told him it had been the best birthday ever. He would later call me with our flight information.

I knew they needed clean clothes after being picked up by the border patrol and held for three days, so I went to Kmart and found luggage and clothes I thought would work.

I drove to the old El Cid hotel, which was once was a large, grand hotel in the 30s and 40s. Now, it was a run-down, dilapidated building, serving a purpose as a fenced holding area for immigrants.

I wanted to get an early start, so I arrived there at 6:00 a.m. While searching for a parking place, I gazed at the hotel with armed guards and a 12-foot-high fence made of steel bars surrounding it. My head was full of questions. I didn't speak Spanish, and I hoped the person at the gate could translate my message to the family.

I parked the car and walked to a small, brick shed, where the guard met me. He spoke English, and I introduced myself, told him I was the sponsor for the family, and gave the court documents over to him, keeping a copy for myself. I handed him the luggage and asked him to deliver it to them. I also explained they needed to be showered, dressed, and ready for me to pick them up at 9:00 a.m. He agreed, but said they were asleep. They could be released at 9:00 a.m. He smiled and quickly turned around and started running.

I walked back to the car. Just as I was opening the car door, I heard screaming from inside the grounds of the hotel. The voices were getting louder. I turned from the car and began walking back towards the gate. Soon, I could see the family standing behind the gate calling my name, reaching for me through the bars with arms and hands waving. . . Each one was jumping up and down and screaming my name. While I reached through the bars of the huge gate, hugging each one, the guard watched and smiled. They recognized me from the pictures Letty had sent to them. They had tears streaming down their faces, laughing and joyful. Staying in America was no longer just a dream— it was coming true. I hugged each one and ask the guard to tell them I was going to leave and return in two hours to take them with me. During that time, I wanted them to shower, change into their new clothes, and get ready for our flight up to San Francisco.

I later learned the guard had woken up the family from a sleepless night. They had been under the impression they were going to be deported back to El Salvador. They were feeling sad and extremely fearful of going back to their war-torn homeland, not knowing where they would be living. Also, they were broke, since they had given the man who assisted them across the border all but just a few dollars. What would they do for food and shelter? The plans to begin a new life in the U.S.A. were seeming to only be a distant dream. That is, until they were alerted to my arrival there.

Back at the hotel, I felt assured and safe to call Letty. She answered, and I said loudly, "I am bringing Alex home to you."

She wasn't sure she heard me right, and said, "Oh, Miss Pat, please repeat what you just said."

I told her again and said, "Your waiting is over. God heard our prayers. I am going to the airport with your family to bring them home to you."

She began to cry and shout with joy. "Oh, Miss Pat, thank you, thank you. I can't believe it. I can't believe it. I must pray now to Jesus." I told her I would be talking to her later. I hung up as she cried and laughed at the same time.

After talking to Letty, I called one of my best friends, Sharon, to plan to meet us at the airport in my station wagon. Sharon was very fond of Letty and happy to be assisting in this joyful celebration.

I went to the dining room, sat down, ordered my food, and bowed my head. I closed my eyes, and I began silently praying, thanking God for delivering Letty's family from the close disaster of being sent back to hell on earth. Instead, He had rescued them. They had a brighter future, a new beginning.

I finished eating, paid my check, and walked to the car. While I was walking, I felt a warm feeling throughout my body. I realized I couldn't feel my feet touching the sidewalk—it was as if I were weightless. I felt a sense of peace, unlike I have ever experienced before. Getting into the car and driving the distance back to the El Cid, I felt relaxed, yet energized. As I drove, I continued to feel comforted. The lingering weight I had carried for months was finally lifted from my shoulders. I had been called to step up and make this happen. Now, my mission was coming to a close, with just a few details left to do.

I turned in the rental car and ordered a shuttle to the airport. The van picked me up and headed to the El Cid hotel. I took out my notebook and began making a list of names to secure employment for the family. I had been ordered by the judge to find jobs for the adults right away. As soon as I arrived home, I would also search the paper for rental homes and jobs.

As soon as the road curved, I could see the family waiting by the gate in the warm, winter sun wearing their new clothes. The clothes draped their bodies. Due to the long ordeal of walking to the border, being picked by the border patrol, and having little food to eat, their clothes were too big.

As the van came to a stop, I got out and helped them get seated. They couldn't stop smiling. Alex had gone to school in Mexico and learned English. I ask him to sit with me, and he was filled with questions—some I could not answer. His beautiful, big, brown eyes were shining. One would say he was beaming with joy.

After talking for a while, I realized they were hungry. I asked the driver to stop at the nearest McDonald's drive-through. We needed something fast to catch our flight on time.

Once we arrived at the airport, they seemed to be more relaxed. We checked in and showed the proper documents. We walked to the gate with boarding passes in hand. Alex—who kept running ahead of us, then stopping to wait for us—was so excited to be on his way to see his mom. He couldn't stand still, jumping up and down. This was his first time on a plane.

Alex buckled his seatbelt, put his face to the window, and watched the activity on the ground. I could see the excitement on his face with takeoff. While flying, he pointed to the snowcapped mountains below. It was his first time to see snow.

Sharon picked up Letty early to make sure to get through traffic and be on time when the plane landed. Once at the gate, Letty moved as close as she could get to the door. As the door opened, she began to cry, watching the passengers one by one as they got off the airplane. In and around the gate, people started to focus on Letty. They knew a special homecoming must be taking place.

Alex realized he was going to see his mom at last. It had been too long. I took his hand, and we walked off the plane with the others behind us. Glancing back at Irma and Miriam, I saw tears in their eyes.

Letty, standing right in front, began to jump up and down, screaming as she saw Alex. Soon, Alex saw her and ran towards her and into her arms. She hugged him, saying his name over and over while swaying back and forth, not wanting to let him go, soaking in the reality that this long-awaited dream was coming true at last.

The other family members surrounded her with hugs. As we made our way to the parking lot, both Sharon and I discussed that neither of us had room for the family to stay in our homes. I suggested we drive to a hotel in a nearby town, where they could stay until I found a house for them to rent.

The next morning, I had appointments to see two houses in the area. I brought the family breakfast and took Letty with me to look at the homes. The first house we looked at had just been published in the newspaper. It was a four-bedroom house with two baths and with major appliances included—it would work. God was still making things happen. It was ready to move in. I signed the lease and paid the deposit and rent. The landlord agreed to allow them to move in the next day. It was still early in the day, so I decided to try my favorite consignment store. I asked to speak to the manager. I met with her and told her about the family just arriving from El Salvador. I needed to purchase four beds, living room furniture, plus a table and chairs. She went the extra mile to get the lowest prices. We found the furniture we needed, and she agreed on next-day delivery.

I brought Letty back to the hotel. Early the next morning, we went to the rental home with cleaning supplies. Letty, her sisters, Alex, and his uncle began cleaning and getting their new home ready to move in. In the meantime, I went for groceries.

My neighbors had heard the news and brought kitchen and bath supplies. The furniture arrived in the afternoon. I went to the store and bought linens and towels. At last, Letty was happy to be with her family in her own home.

I began to call friends about employing the girls as housekeepers. By the end of the week, they had jobs. I called my friend at Big Boy restaurant and asked him if he needed a dishwasher. I warned him that the man didn't speak English. He said bring him over to interview the next day.

At the end of the next day, my friend called and said, "Even though he doesn't speak English, that doesn't stop him from being a hard worker. He is hired." Three weeks went by, and my friend called to say he let his two other dishwashers go—this man ran circles around them.

Alex enrolled in school. He loved sports and was a good student. Eventually, he graduated from high school with honors. He went on to college. Alex is in now in sales and has worked for the same company for over 20 years. He and his wife have two children. They have purchased a beautiful home with a guest suite. Letty lives with them and helps take care of her grandchildren. She is very happy.

The sisters have their own homes and are living the American Dream. All of the family members now have citizenship papers. Within five years, they had reimbursed me for the court costs. This experience inspired me to reach out and help others. My favorite passage from the Bible is Philippians 4:13, "I can do all things through Jesus Christ, who strengthens me."

MY SPIRIT, MY SOUL

Day to day, year to year, and little by little,
My body changes, giving way to gravity,
and youth is left behind.
A new beginning, a new dawning is rising.
And my soul awakens to the inner being.
Feelings stir deep within, and I search outward,
upward, to the Creator.
No longer does the rush occur, but gives in to an honest heart,
feeling of emotion swell of love and goodness to each creature I behold .
My soul is nurtured with milk and honey, and
warmed with spiritual light of feelings worthy of the day
to come, to go forward, like a new beginning.
My spirit, my soul, stay warmed and connected
to run the race of bravery and sever the strings of fear.
Never hinder the paths of tomorrow.
Take the wisdom of today and calm the storms of tomorrow.
I need not, but only the need to stir the desires of another to reach out
for his new beginnings, then my life will cease to search for meaning.
My spirit, my soul, compose thy dignity with tranquility and serenity
to rest and wait on tomorrow, to stir the desire of another,
till the Almighty Creator summons my soul
for again a new beginning.

Patricia Laub
Published by
The National Library of POETRY 1995

HISTORY & RESUME:
PATRICIA J. LAUB- 2020

1971-2020 Resided in Orinda, Ca.

Married to ARNOLD LAUB, lawyer Mother of 5 children (3 step-children) Attended Orinda Presbyterian Church

Served as co-chairman of Festival of Trees, for American Cancer Society 1972 San Francisco, Ca.

President of the local Women's Republican Club 1973

President of the Orinda Women's Club 1974

EMPLOYMENT HISTORY

Director of Marketing & Public Relations -A. Laub Office, S.F. Ca. 1977-1984

Achievements: Provided effective PR and Marketing strategies that resulted in growing business from (1) office to 10) offices throughout California.

Wrote and edited test for successful TV commercials which increased client base.

Property Manager 1977-Present

Real Estate Sales - Blackhawk Realty 1985-1990 Crisis Counselor, Contra Costa County Crisis Center John Kennedy University, Pleasant Hill, Ca.

1993-1997 Degree in Psychology Relocated to Miami, Oklahoma 1999 Member of First Methodist, Miami Owned & operated PJ Laub Properties

Served on the board of Ottawa County Crisis Center. 2000

Chairman for 4 years of Festiv al of Trees to benefit the Crises Center. (First year netted $2,400. final year netted $92,000. 2001-2005.

2004 General Contractor,to planning & building, overseeing personal residence 4,000 sq.ft. Structure. On 200 acres. Afton, Ok.

2005 to present purchased & flipped houses.

2015 Sold residence. Purchased home in Miami, Ok 2016 Joined New Life Nazarene Church

2020 Wrote & published a book "Letty's Do or Die Courage.

CPSIA information can be obtained
at www.ICGtesting.com
Printed in the USA
LVHW101641050121
675305LV00081B/198

9 781952 884207